Conversations with Juliet

Management and Leadership Skills, Learnt from a Child

Martin Haworth is a coach, trainer and business writer with extensive management experience. For over 25 years, he managed teams ranging in size from 6 to 300 in various challenging environments. He now works with major organisations to help them bring out the best of their management teams, as well as individuals, who want to enhance and develop their management skills. He lives in Gloucester, England and has no pets.

***

For a unique pack of bonus articles to complement this book, go to martinhaworth.com/extras-1 or on the bonus page at the end!

And if you love the book, do me the favour of giving it a review, I'd really appreciate it.

Thank you and enjoy!

Martin Haworth

Table of Contents

Chapter 1 - Endings

As the fanfare started up - the music to announce the final results - the giant spotlight flashed around the room. Seated heads bobbed up and down excitedly, and the chatter volume increased. This was the culmination of a lot of hard work and above all, the final analysis for the contestants.

For a moment, Michael saw the focus of the light hover on Suzanne, seated just across the aisle from him, and Michael considered the fascinating year she had experienced.

Just 12 months ago, they sat down together to complete her performance review and it was less than good. Suzanne, despite the meteoric rise in her career up to now, just hadn't shown she had what it takes in a larger store and her performance and that of her business had, so far, been disappointing.

It had been starting to get to her in the meeting that day, and Michael had pondered whether she might find the going sufficiently tough to give it all up. It would be a disappointment, but sometimes that happened.

But tonight she was up for that most challenging of titles with her team. She was in the final six for the Store of the Year, which, considering there were over 800 units in the business as a whole, was remarkable in itself. More remarkable was the real expectation around the place that she and her team might just pull it off.

Over the past year the performance of her team had become exceptional, and it seemed to start just after mid-summer. So fascinated had Michael been with the startling turnaround, that, as his divisional winner, he had taken Suzanne and her team out to dinner, just a week ago, to try to find out more.

Purposefully, he had arranged the seating so that he sat between Suzanne and one of her team leaders, Rosie, especially so that he could try to understand better where this stunning change in performance had come from.

Chapter 2 - Beginnings

Suzanne began the story just a year earlier, at a barbecue that she attended at Rosie's house...

"It was a beautiful summer's day in early August, and I remember vividly that I almost didn't go. Rosie is a good friend of mine, as well as one of my team leaders.

We'd been having a tough time at work, and she had been quite down about how things had been going. In my position, I was doing my best to really push the team. Because of that, our relationship had begun to suffer. Despite the fact that I'd been to her home on many occasions, I wasn't sure whether she might want a bit of a breather from me.

The decider for me was the call that David, her husband, made to Steve, my partner, which meant that they would need to meet to discuss a business deal that they were doing together - so I knew that I would need to be there with him.

Once we arrived, I was glad I had gone, because Rosie was on great form and it was good to speak to so many people that I knew and gradually, I started to relax during the round of introductions and small talk.

Just as I was settling in, Rosie's daughter, Juliet, marched determinedly over to say 'Hi'.

Juliet is a precocious eight-year old who is an absolute darling. She looked just lovely in the colourful summer dress, which as she told me proudly - and in a way that only little girls can - was brand new for the event. She had obviously taken her hostess duties very seriously.

In the next 15 minutes, I was to begin a journey which would take me from the depths of my business despair, to the success I and my team have had over the last year..........and Juliet was the trigger, provider and facilitator of all the action that was to take place.

She took my hand and we walked down towards the lake, which was at the bottom of their garden. The house in which they lived was quite modest, but a few shrewd business deals that David had pulled off had enabled them to build in a wonderful location by the lake.

She sat me down on a seat made between two tree stumps and I basked in the delight of a beautiful day, a delightful view and above all, the opportunity to spend a little time with Juliet.

The conversation went like this: -

"So Juliet, how are you? You look very beautiful today."

Smoothing the front of her dress carefully, Juliet was clearly proud of it and unexpectedly said, "I love my Mummy a lot you know."

"Of course you do, and you know that your Mummy loves you too." I replied.

"Well, I think she does, but sometimes I don't really know."

I'd spent enough time with Juliet over the last few years to know that this was one bright child. It would not be just a fleeting thought that had led to a comment like this.

"How can that be? Surely, she loves you all the time," and after a moment's thought I added, "When you say sometimes, when is it that she doesn't love you?"

"Sometimes when she's tired, she tells me off." She said looking thoughtfully around her.

Leaping to my long time friend's defence, I said, "Well all Mummies get a little tired from time to time. They have a lot to do, you know. Have you noticed when is she tired most?" I asked, determined to get to the bottom of this unexpected conversation.

"Usually it's the days when she comes home from work," said Juliet, throwing a rock into the lake, thoughtfully.

My mind slipped into thinking about the occasions recently where we had been short in our teams, and we'd all had to work extra to make up. It was not an imposed decision from me, but because we were a close team, everyone pulled together and did a shift or two extra each month.

It had been hard for me too, and I dreaded to think about what it must have been like for those with families. Steve and I had a few moments of real disagreement recently, which was unusual for us.

"And is she always tired when she comes home from work?" I added, gently.

"No, just sometimes." Juliet ran over to whisper something in the ear of another little girl and they both looked towards a boy of their own age, who was standing close to his father. They giggled and she ran back to me.

I felt as though I was on a mission now, so I needed to ask her, "Apart from when she tells you off, how can you tell she's tired?"

"Sometimes she cries and gets angry," Juliet said with a distressed look on her face - the smile she brought back from the giggles with her friend had now disappeared.

"With you?" I started to feel that twinge in my stomach once more. She'd already mentioned 'work', so was this something to do with me?

"Yes sometimes, but mainly with things at work."

So here it was, work stuff was the thing. I needed to know more about this, the effect my involvement in work was having on real people, people that I loved, but I was driving in a way which wasn't truly who I was.

"How do you mean, with work?"

Juliet thought for a moment and then said, "Well, when she's angry with something that's happened at work and she tells Daddy all about it, sometimes she cries."

I felt a lump come to my throat as I asked her, "What is it about work that makes Mummy cry?"

"She gets angry and cries because she says she doesn't matter at work, even though she tries so hard - I know she does, because she's my Mummy."

This was coming from the daughter of a close friend; from the mother of this child. The workplace I had control of was having this effect on her. And I also recalled that I had been affected myself - hence the rows with Steve.

I now saw myself becoming defensive, and to an eight-year old child as well, as I asked, "What does she mean that she doesn't matter at work?"

"Well, she doesn't tell me so much, she just wipes her tears away and says that it doesn't matter, but I hear her telling Daddy."

"What does she say to Daddy?"

"That even when she tries hard, people don't say thank you, or make her feel like she's doing a good job."

I could understand that. Since my move to this much larger business, I had felt challenged. In the past I'd been able to keep control myself; be 'hands on'; be a do-er, but now, in this far larger environment, I'd tried so hard to do just that and keep everything mine - I had been afraid of doing things differently.

I'd missed taking the team with me, and valuing them as people. A talent I'd always prided myself on, ever since I began my management career.

"And does that make her sad?" I persisted. Now biting the bullet, I was really determined to get to the bottom of the very real challenges the whole of this family (and others in my team) were facing – especially if I was implicated.

"Yes, that's when she cries sometimes."

"And how does that make you feel, Juliet?"

"I feel sad too and try to make her feel better, but I can't."

"What do you do?" I said, fearing what was to come next.

"I hold her hand and give her a hug, but sometimes she cries more."

I have to admit it, at this point a couple of tears welled up in my eyes at the efforts a little girl was making to make things better for her mother. I had never quite realised the impact that work life had on other people. My fast-track career progress had dulled my senses and held me away from the real world. I had become more focused on the outcomes and not the **way** to do things.

"Do you know why she goes to work, Juliet?" I asked quietly.

"To make sure that we all have nice things to wear and so that we can go on holidays like my other friends. And when Daddy wasn't working last year, she helped to pay the bills."

I remembered that David had had an accident, and being self-employed had found a spell when he was unable to work, nor bring in any income. Things were OK now, at least in some ways.

I had always had a belief that part of my role as a 'boss' was to ensure that my people had an attachment to work such that they went home each night wanting to come back the next day.

Maybe it was an exceptional challenge, but since I felt that it must be right, I then asked Juliet, "Does she not like going to work?"

She looked over to her mother, who was busy unwrapping salads and all the other dishes to accompany the barbecue. David reappeared from behind a cloud of smoke as the barbecue began its real work of delivering the hot food.

"I don't think she does now - she used to do. But now, it seems different and she isn't excited about it like she was before - I think she sort of hates going to work. It makes Daddy feel sad too."

And so we now had a full suite of the family involved, Dad was hurting too. "How do you know it makes Daddy feel sad?" I asked.

In a considered way (at least it was for an eight-year old), Juliet said, "Because he tells me that he wishes that Mummy didn't need to go to work there anymore."

"So why doesn't she stop?" I said, half wondering out loud to myself in question, but also directed towards Juliet.

Almost without thinking, Juliet said, "Because she likes the people there and she says that if she stopped, she'd miss the people she works with. I think she always feels that it is so close to being better - so close - and that's why she keeps trying."

Determined to get right to the bottom of this, I then asked Juliet, "So why does she not like it now?"

"I think it's because she thinks she's not worth much there and that she isn't ap, ap, ap...what is that word?" she said, a little frustrated.

"Appreciated," I offered, and Juliet nodded. "So why on earth does she think that?" I asked in desperation, because I dearly loved the members of my team and this just wasn't the outcome of our work together that I expected, nor intended.

Now frustrated herself, Juliet replied, "Because no-one tells her and no-one gives her new things to learn. She says they haven't enough time to do it all. She says that no-one listens to her or the others when they have their own ideas and solutions."

Enough information, I thought, and then one last question flipped into my mind, "What would you like your Mummy to do Juliet?"

"I just want her to be happy and to love me all the time when she's here."

So that was quite simple really, wasn't it?

As Steve and I drove home, I was thinking hard and wondering how I'd got myself into this position and how, or even if, I could recover.

Steve knew I was worried - not quite with it. He has always had a great sense of intuition and he asked me what was wrong.

I started to tell him about my experience with Juliet and as I spoke, I was picturing her face and what I felt I had done to help create that confusion and upset. What I now needed to do to resolve it.

This was going to take more than a bit of thought, and, little though I knew it, the opportunity to make a start would arrive more quickly than I might have expected.

Chapter 3 - Communication

I have always helped out Rosie and David by babysitting for them every month or so, so they could have a night out together. By chance, I was due to go over there two nights later to look after Juliet and her brother, Miles.

I wasn't too sure that I could handle another bout of Juliet for the moment, but I knew how much her parents looked forward to some time to themselves.

So as I walked in the door, said my 'Hellos' to everyone, and then my 'see you laters' to Rosie and David, I was part fascinated and part apprehensive about how my evening with Juliet would go.

It was time to sit down and listen to Juliet read to me, which she had done since she could, so the plan was for her to read the bedtime book to me and her brother, Miles. I asked him to switch down the TV so that they could hear the story.

The TV was in the corner and I could see it out of the corner of my eye. An item appeared on there as she began reading and my attention was drawn to the TV for a split second.

My eyes wandered.

Immediately, Juliet said, "I like it best when Mummy listens carefully to me when I am reading - and doesn't watch the television at the same time!" Point taken. So I switched the TV off and listened carefully to the rest of the story.

Miles, being the younger of the two, went to bed first and then I had the opportunity to talk to Juliet on her own. The issue of 'Mummy listening' had clearly been of importance to her, so I asked her what else there was about when Mummy listened to her that she noticed.

It took her less than one minute to tell me the important things about being listened to and they were as follows: -

"Well, when she looks at me I know she's really listening to me and is interested because she asks me about what I'm telling her. She smiles and nods her head a lot and she doesn't do anything else." Like watch the television, I thought. I was suitably admonished!

Juliet carried on, "If she gets interrupted, she says sorry and tries to stop it happening again, and she always remembers if she has had to break off when I'm telling her something.

"I feel Mummy is really, really interested in me and if she hasn't time or is not really able to listen properly, she tells me why, and we do it later. And when she talks to me I can always understand what she says."

So there you have it!

This was so simple and yet so profound at the same time.

It was not until my drive home that it started to hit me, that this was precisely what I was not doing with my team.

I was so excited thinking through where I had been missing out with them and what I could now do, that I decided to make myself some notes before I went to bed and prepare for tomorrow, when I could put what I'd learnt into practice.

There were plenty of opportunities for me, because I had formal and informal conversations with people every day, but I really wanted to use this in a constructive way for the first time with someone who would be open to a change in my style. That would give me the confidence to go on in the future.

Rosie had already asked for some time with me over the next few days and I knew it would be a tricky conversation. As pressure had built up over the last few months, and despite our closeness, we had had our moments where the stress had got in my way. This would be the time to bring her closer to me, and share where we were going together.

I took a few preparatory steps.

Firstly, I made sure that my desk and office were tidy of all clutter and that I could ensure that I would not be disturbed – I would pull the plug out of my phone – after telling the switchboard I was going to be busy for an hour. I switched my pager off and wrote a note asking for some privacy, and then I stuck it neatly in the window of my office door.

Once I got this far, there were other things that came to mind about communication. Of how I thought at first, the importance of communicating with people was to get a message across, and then I reflected further. Maybe it was more about ensuring that the recipient received what I wanted them to receive. Which was different.

The discussion went well. So much so that Rosie said words of appreciation as she left.

"You know Suzanne, it's been great that you made the time to really hear what I had to say. I do feel that we've been fully together this afternoon and we're on the right road again, after some months without a clear direction. It's great to have you back – and any help I can give you, you only need to ask."

"I'd love to have some feedback from our conversation this afternoon," I said, "Just few minutes."

"Well, I feel that you have really listened to me today, that you share my concerns fully and that you've been prepared to give me your full attention. I think that there's much more to you than I thought – and I knew you pretty well already. You've recovered the old form, the old you I knew before and it's so good to see."

And I had listened. I had made real space, which she'd deeply appreciated. I'd recovered a bit and built rapport – much better than I had been doing.

Later in the day I had some other feedback from one of the team. It had been necessary to pin up a notice to explain a new procedure. Things had not gone to plan and we had got a real mouthful from one of our auditors.

When I started to look more closely, I asked a couple of people involved and they told me that they had done exactly what had been asked of them.

I couldn't understand what had gone wrong at all. Until we went through my instructions line by line, step by step.

There was one sentence that made clear sense to me – very clear. Yet, somehow, the interpretation of what I had written had not been the same for them as it had been when I wrote it. They had read something different to what I'd said. Or I meant to say.

I wasn't aware of what I'd said that was wrong, yet the result we'd achieved was unacceptable – and I'd learnt some lessons about my communication.

Lessons which I would come to value significantly, over the months to come.

My Key Points on Communication

Listen and Be Present

By completely focusing on people, I am able to fully 'listen' to what is being said when they are talking to me. I found this to be beneficial in my relationships with my team. Indeed sometimes, I got a hint at some things that they weren't quite able to say and prompt them to be open with me.

Is Your Message Getting Across?

Checking that what I said to people is what they really heard became one of my priorities. I realised that what I said might be heard as a very different message than I thought I was putting out. I now know that responsibility lies with me to check this and set up ways of finding out just what has been their understanding of my message.

Make the Time

When I 'cleared' time for my discussion with Rosie I could tell it made a big, big difference to our relationship and allowed me to explore 'in the moment' her concerns. I am now more at ease to make time both formally **and** informally too, to really get to know people better.

Ask Questions

By listening to what people say and asking good open questions, both about what I hear and what I want to know, has often given me valuable and sometimes unexpected information, and I know it has made my colleagues feel very listened to because, like Rosie, they have told me.

Use Simple Language

Why over-complicate things? One of the great assets I was able to develop was learning to talk common sense and other people's language. More and more I catch myself cutting through the jargon and getting practical.

Chapter 4 - Leadership

It was time for the ballet school performance. This was a once a year event for the little (and not so little!) girls and boys who attended the 'Miss Greer School of Ballet and Dance'. If that sounded a formal title, well it was – and Miss Greer ran the school with the proverbial rod of steel.

I was attending rehearsals as a helper, mainly because when I'd been a little girl, this was where I had learnt all about my own 'pliés' and 'pas de deux'. And I had loved every minute of it. I still went to the adult tap classes most Tuesday evenings and the place had become an important part of my life.

As I grew older even fierce Miss Greer became more tolerable, more understanding and now, I hold her in the highest regard.

Tonight was the final evening before the show – the final dress rehearsal - and everyone was on their best behaviour.

Miss Greer took to the floor, centre-stage and everyone was quiet and watching, very intently.

"What do we want to do tomorrow night?"

"Anyone?"

A small hand appeared towards the back of the crowd of dancers. "Yes. Who is that? Come forward."

I might have guessed, it was Juliet!

"Miss Greer." She said, quite confidently, as she walked through to the front.

"Miss Greer. We want a fabulous performance, where everyone does their best and above all, that we all have such fun!"

Miss Greer looked closely at Juliet. Her hair was up in a tight bun, which rather ominously, quivered slightly.

"We want a fabulous performance, where everyone does their best and above all, that we all have such fun!"

"What does anyone else think?"

Silence.

The group had reached the point, as they had often done with Miss Greer, where they really weren't sure what the best answer would be.

"Weeell?" She asked, intently.

"I think Juliet is quite right." said another small child, over to the right of the stage. Others chimed in now too. "Lots of fun." "Do our best." "Fabulous performance."

All came as garbled and excited comments from the crowd of motivated kids.

"Absolutely right." said Miss Greer. "If we have some fun (only some, mind you!), and you all do your best, we will have a 'Fabulous Performance'. Are we all very, very clear about that?"

The resounding response was a definite and rousing, 'YES'.

"Now, my job tonight and tomorrow night is to help you make these things happen. So as of tonight, I am not your teacher any longer. I am here to make everything run smoothly for each of you, so that you can do the best job you can tomorrow night. You are the only ones that can do it. I am here for you."

With that, there was silence and then, slowly at first, there was applause. Every single member of the class rose to their feet and gave Miss Greer the most tremendous round of applause they could.

"And now I need a cup of tea!" With that, Miss Greer pirouetted off the stage and was heard to be discussing - at some length with the dress designer - how much extra material would be needed for Belinda's frock, so that she could dance the 'Swan Lake' just perfectly!

The following night was not perfect. But it was great!

After the show, I was behind the scenes, listening to the excited chatter as the girls and boys re-enacted the night's events. When Miss Greer came in, there were cheers and flowers and, was that a little tear or two that I noticed in her eye? Probably!

So, how could I apply this back at the store?

Although I felt that the behaviour that I had seen in Miss Greer was very fundamental, I hadn't worked out the link yet with what it could be described as in the store.

However, the opportunity was just around the corner....

We were quite stuck in the way forward. I had realised it for several weeks, and yet it had taken that evening with Miss Greer (with a little help from Juliet, of course!) to realise what it was I needed to do to truly lead from the front as their Leader.

The key point was that we didn't know where we were going; what we wanted the business to truly be. The time had come for some clear thinking – so, a special meeting (with pizzas!) was called for.

There was a great place down through the town by the waterfront and as had happened before, we would meet up there, just the key players, once in a while, to toss things around and have a think about stuff without the distraction of the business.

I felt that although the business was important, taking some time to work **on** the business rather than **in** the business was just as vital too.

On time, (for the pizzas were just great!), the team assembled and a few of the junior staff were asked to join together with us too.

You see, I hate to be seen as elitist, with just the 'favoured' few in attendance, so in this case it was necessary to cascade down my vision for the business and we asked more than usual. But the numbers still needed to be kept down at this stage of planning, if just to keep this reasonably manageable.

As they settled down, I remembered the key activity for tonight was to share with them the 'what' and not the 'how' – otherwise I would end up with most of the 'doing' myself and leave the team out of it. Which would be no good for any of us.

"I wanted to get together tonight because I need to share how I'm feeling about the business and I need your help to get things focused." I began slowly, on purpose.

"I have a view for the future of this Store which I want to share with you and I hope that you will join me in ensuring that we agree, and that we work together to deliver what I see as a vision of the way forward.

"I have four key areas where I think we want to be the best: -

- We become famous for being absolutely the best at giving our customers a memorable experience.

- We have a second-to-none record for stock availability on our shelves.

- We set ourselves standards of operating our business better than similar businesses both inside and outside the organisation.

- We look after our own people in every way we can to enable them to grow, develop and want to come to work each day.

"These are my visions for the future of our business. It would really help if you would throw some thoughts at this for the rest of the evening."

There was a hubbub of chatter as each of those present warmed up to the issues, especially as I'd prepared written details to replicate what I'd said verbally, which I passed around.

After 15 minutes of discussion, one of the team leaders got up slowly and said to the group. "I think this is a great way to push us forward. I'd love to be able to take this back to my people to ask them not just what they think, but also how we can work as a group to deliver this fantastic goal for the business."

Others joined in and overall, I was so delighted at how well my thoughts had been received.

Another replied, "At last we can see what you are asking from us and now it will be so much easier for us to use this as a target to aim at. In my team we will be able to measure everything we know against this vision for the business. We'll be behind it and think of it as a great plan to work on and deliver together."

I'd been pleased at the response so far, so now it was time to ramp it up. Remembering what I'd seen in Miss Greer and Juliet, I followed through what I now realised to be another key point of leadership and as the energy gradually ran out in the room, I stepped up once again.

"The vision I have shared with you for the future of this business here is a first step. As I see it, my role now is to enable it to happen through you. I have made some mistakes over the last few months and I am ready to acknowledge that.

"What I want you to help me with now, is to understand how best I can help you deliver this vision. I am not going to be able to do this on my own and I want to help you all get fully involved in delivering this big challenge I have for the Store.

"I want to help you, but also understand how much I value each and every one of the team...to help you all by getting out of your hair and smoothing the path to your success. I will commit to give you each the skills to deliver this goal and to support you if things go wrong a bit."

Everyone was paying very close attention indeed. The whole team, including the junior staff, seemed fully engaged as I was speaking. It was the combination of a clear vision for the future and the passion I was trying to inject that had them enthralled.

"I want this to be a safe and creative place and if I feel that you are taking a wrong direction I will share that with you without judgment. I will find ways to get the resources to help you with the challenge even if I have to fight for them myself. We will work together to support the development of the individual teams and the overall team within the Store.

"I'd like us all to agree that the way we work together in the future always ensures that we value our life outside the business, and I haven't done as well as I could in this, even for myself, and that will change – my intention is for all of us."

I sensed much approval and I could see some nodding of heads around the table on this one – clearly an important point for them all.

I continued, "And when we succeed in delivering this ambitious challenge, we will have the party to beat all parties, I promise you that!"

Well, after that, in a pizza place down by the waterside, I received the first ever, standing ovation heard there. Every one of the key members of my team present that evening were alongside me – all in it together!

The challenge was not just on, they were up there with me, straining at the leash to get started.

My Key Points on Leadership

Create a Vision

Where I could, I included them to work with me **with** me on the vision for the future. So I became open – **we** became open - to the challenges ahead – and also from where we were starting from and where the gap was – that's where we did our best work.

Be Very Honest

It was tough at first, but I've started to share with the team my fears and concerns. To share my dreams and hopes for the future. They loved being included. So we went for the occasional off-line day (or a pizza!) to talk things through in the space we needed.

Be a 'What' not a 'How' leader

With a clear goal and expressed expectations (the 'what'), I finally 'got' that it's a good thing to let people find out the best way to deliver the result (the 'how'). I realised that I cannot do it for them to get the very best results. Nor can I build team morale and commitment if I get them up for the challenge and then do it all for them.

Deliver the Result

Acknowledging that my job as a leader is to ensure the result gets delivered - and that alone - was an eye-opener for me. I saw that my role was to make conditions such that my people could deliver the outcomes we agreed and give them the space to do it.

Model the Best Behaviours

Great leaders have a balanced life. They take breaks, holidays etc. They see their kids in their Sports Days. I try hard to show them that it's just fine to have a life outside work and value that. Achieving our vision will be quite a journey, and everyone needs to be need to be healthy, motivated and sharp.

Be Fair and Consistent

I think that as I grew with the challenge, we created an environment where everyone pulls together and trusts each other. I had to be extremely careful with my own integrity here, taking care to notice where I was showing favour – or otherwise. I had to ensure that I treated everyone equally to get the best from the whole team.

Chapter 5 - Meetings

Juliet had given me a couple of great lessons and I couldn't wait for the next babysitting session, and even more that I could share the success I had experienced, with my new 'mentor'.

It was much to my disappointment though, that when I arrived at Juliet's house, she was nowhere to be seen. Indeed Rosie told me that Juliet was in her bedroom having been distressed earlier that evening at Brownies.

When I asked what the problem had been, Rosie didn't seem to know; just that Juliet had flounced in, very tearfully and had said she was going to bed, and that she wanted nothing to do with anyone for the rest of the evening!

Well, you can imagine just how I felt with Juliet being out of the picture for my evening - it was a bit like being stood up by a new boyfriend! As before, Rosie and David went out - this time it was to a PTA event at Juliet's school. So I settled down to read to Miles, Juliet's brother and ponder on my lowered expectations for the evening.

After about half an hour, I tucked Miles up in his bed and started to creep downstairs. There was not a sound from Juliet's room, so my last chance to share my success was off for tonight. Or so I thought.

I went back downstairs and through the kitchen to collect the supper, which Rosie always left for me when I was looking after the kids. I stepped from the kitchen into the lounge and almost jumped out of my skin as Juliet was sitting quietly on the sofa, looking at me. I could see she was bleary eyed and still a little upset, with those almost imperceptible shivers that children do after a crying bout.

"Hey." I said to Juliet and I got a "Hey to you too," back. And a smile!

It was good to see her perking up, if only a little. Although I wanted to find out what she had been so upset about, I thought it best to settle things down further first of all, so I made a bit of small talk.

"How've you been, Juliet?" I asked her.

Again she looked a little more hopeful for me as she said, "Cool - well, pretty cool anyway."

"And what have you been up to?"

"I'm very upset, actually," she said, in a very grown-up way, which almost made me smile. You know how that can happen when someone else is just so serious and then says something really seriously. Your mind sort of flips and you get a fit of the giggles - and then what do you do?

I faked a cough!

"How's that?" I asked her

"Well, we had a terrible time at Brownies this evening and I'm not going again!"

"What was so awful about it then Juliet?" I asked sympathetically.

"Well, every so often we have a meeting about what we are going to do over the next term, and we decide the things we think the group will like to do – but the meetings are always terrible, with everyone shouting and really, really disorganized – I don't know why I ever get asked, no-one ever listens to me anyway."

31

She went on, "We are never clear about what we are there for, some of us don't get the chance to speak and then if we do, a couple of the others always say what we have said is 'stupid', or just laugh out loud and I feel like a fool."

I thought about this for a moment, "So, you aren't clear why you are going along to the meeting before you go. And when you go it's very disorganized and then no-one is interested in what you have to say?"

"Yes, and then at the end it always goes on longer than it should and Daddy is kept waiting, and then no-one is sure who is doing what to organize things either and then it gets left to the last minute in a panic to get things organized when the time comes."

Phew!

I said, after a faint glimmer of recognition, somewhere deep inside me, "It really upset you didn't it Juliet?"

"Yes, it did and it's not the first time either – it makes me feel like I don't want to go along any more. It leaves a bad feeling, which spoils the rest of the time I'm there at our normal meetings."

I gave her a hug and reflected on what she had said. Perhaps I was being more aware after the progress I had made with my team, after Juliet's recent 'shares', but it did make me think. Perhaps there was something more that I could learn from this bright and bubbly 8-year old.

The next day was my regular meeting with the team from my division. This involved a 25-mile drive to the Divisional office, where there would be about 18-20 colleague managers in attendance.

These were not particularly well organized and most of the group of managers who attended didn't feel there was much value to them, so I thought I'd apply the issues that Juliet had raised for herself and see just where the sensitive points were.

The divisional team leader was my immediate boss, Michael, and he was in charge of getting the meeting going. As usual, we didn't know what the meeting was to be about and although there was a vague pattern, it varied as Michael attempted to stimulate interest and create motivation in the troops.

The meeting was set for 9.30 until 12.30 and as usual it was 9.50 before we got started and even then a couple of stragglers came in late. Mobile phones kept going off and people were in and out of the room taking calls – this went on all morning really and was particularly annoying for the others. It was only a couple of people who behaved in this way, but nonetheless, it was still a pain.

The agenda was passed around and most of us were asking each other, in a general hubbub of noise, what certain topics were about. This was the usual ploy – ask someone else what the topics were in the vain hope that someone else knew.

I had once been to a meeting where I had absolutely nothing to do with the topic and when I discussed it with Michael afterwards, he said it was 'good for my development'. Hmm.

Michael tried to gain order amid the chaos and gradually most of us came to heel and paid attention (there were still quite a lot of asides though, which were still very distracting).

"There are three changes to the agenda. The topic on 'Budgets' will be scrapped; the one on 'Health and

Safety' will also be cancelled, as I need more information.

"In addition there will be a review of the 'Forward Planning' topic, from last time, which will mean the meeting will need to be extended until 2 o'clock. "

A mobile phone rang to break the numbing silence. This was hardly 'leading by example'.

For the next two hours, the meeting progressed. It was the usual arguing between attendees, talking across each other, often three separate conversations going on at once.

Sometimes there were very vociferous debates and ideas were easily quashed with, well, nothing less than the rudeness that bullies show when they can shout loudest, or, more importantly when they are always right and stuck in their one-track thinking.

Some people talked almost every time and then there were others, especially one woman who hadn't been before who looked around puzzled with the look of fear like a rabbit caught in the headlights.

We stopped for a break, with some rushing for their mobiles and others, even worse, collecting their e-mails on their laptops. I caught up with the new manager, who was attending for the first time.

"How are you doing?" I asked, trying to show at least one small bit of support on her first attendance.

"Well, I feel totally confused – there are lots of bits of jargon I don't understand, I've not been able to ask a couple of questions that might have clarified things a bit for me and, well, this is a total shambles, isn't it?"

I felt rather embarrassed actually, because she was so right. We, as a group had accepted this style of meeting and had become so close to it that it had become the norm.

There had to be a better way.

The meeting got underway again, with Michael refusing questions, as he was already behind, even the new schedule.

The meeting wore on and as we approached the 2pm deadline, there was little sign of completion, and I was starving.

In the end we wrapped up by 2.35.

No-one was really sure what was going to happen next. Michael himself seemed to be taking care of the things that now needed action. This usually happened but there was no real follow up and things just fell over the edge, sometimes never to be seen or heard of again.

We wrapped up late, with no time for questions and for my new friend, with little opportunity to get involved.

It was all well and good to criticise, but when was I going to get my own act together, I asked myself?

Each Monday I held a team meeting where we discussed business performance and issues of the moment. There was always a reluctance to come to these, with the key players often making excuses.

The meeting ran on sometimes for 3 hours and I knew from the past, and had even felt it myself, that there were times when the majority felt totally bored.

So how could I take my new skills - courtesy of Juliet and my observations of Michael's meeting - forward?

Well, there was no place to start like the beginning, so this week I planned ahead (now there was a novelty in itself!) for the meeting on the following Monday.

If I was having a clean start, it seemed a great opportunity to do a little more than to impose a whole new set of stuff on the team – it felt better to let them hear what I had been thinking about and to have a say themselves.

I wasn't sure exactly what that would be like for me, as I had always been 'in charge', but it wasn't working, so it could do no harm to change.

My first step was to explain my thoughts to them at our next meeting, so I devised a simple agenda, which I had ready to e-mail to them by the previous Friday afternoon, to give them chance to think about it beforehand.

In circulating it, I explained a little that this was a bit of a different approach if they would bear with me I would explain a little more at the meeting.

My agenda looked like this:-

Introductions
- New people
- New meeting process

Meeting Objectives and Others' Expectations
- Complete the work
- Make the agreed times

- Have some fun
- Feel involved
- Be aware upfront about potential 'Any Other Business' and try to cover during the meeting

Ground Rules
- Agree collaboratively
- Keep on track
- Value each other
- No speaking across each other
- One conversation

Agenda Items
- Business Performance
    - Staff costs
    - Sales
    - Stockholding issues
    - Stock losses
- Christmas Planning
- Team incentives
- Town Carnival float

Action Points and Commitments

- Who is doing what, by when?

- Who is circulating the notes and commitments from the meeting, and by when?

Review of the Meeting
- What had been good about the meeting
- What we could do differently to make it even better next time

Hey, this felt good. All I had to do was try it out and get buy in. So that's exactly what I did with the team.

We have been holding our meetings like this for a few weeks now and you know, they aren't perfect at all. But they are getting there. I asked a couple of the folks to say what it was about them that was better.

"Things get done now"

"We trust each other much more and listen to others great ideas"

"The meetings finish on time"

"I can really get into the meeting now, whereas in the past I kept having to rush out – now I delegate for others to cover for me"

"You know, I think we all make better decisions now, because we can all throw in our ideas without one or two giving the impression that the rest of us are useless"

For me, I've had to learn a lot about myself and let go of control more. I'm not as 'in charge'' now, and that has been a bit of a challenge for me to let go of. The upside has been considerable for me. I have seen already:-

- A contributory side to people I didn't know they had in them

- A collaborative style emerge in our meetings

- Things get done

- A keenness to attend, both because things happen and also because things start and finish on time

- My sometimes delegating the leading of the meeting – which has been really powerful for me – I can sit back and get in there with my team rather than be up front as 'the boss'

- The meetings are getting better each week as we review how we have done

- The meetings are getting shorter (I found out that meetings are a **lot** less effective after 90 minutes), as we start to understand the things which are nice to debate rather than need to be debated – stuff gets passed round to share - in advance - rather than take up valuable meeting time

- People feel valued because everyone's expectations are heard and acted upon

My Key Points on Meetings

The Right People

No-one wants to waste time at the wrong meeting, so I started to make sure that whoever attends needs to be there and that all who do attend are valuable assets to have there. Excluding some might have hurt a bit to start with, but enabled me to share the message of using everyone's time to best value.

Agree Ground Rules

At the beginning of the meeting we now make sure that everyone agrees ground rules which value and focus everyone's attention. My example above is one way to do this, but we also allow people to decide – for the team - a template for on-going use. Together we make sure to honour time expectations effectively.

Have a Clear Agenda and Objectives

Nowadays we circulate an agenda at least 24 hours ahead and are all clear what the purpose and intended outcomes of the meeting are. If anyone else has specific things they want to be raised – we try to have some slack for that, but not too much. Once agreed, (most times!), we stick to our agenda.

Honour Each Other

There are no wrong answers. As my own feedback shows, people evolve and start to shine when they are allowed to. We encourage our meetings to be a safe and creative place by honouring **everyone's** input as valuable.

Create Accountabilities

At the end of the meeting have we always have agreed Action points, which individuals sign up to and deliver to a timescale. Circulated at the end of the meeting or within 24 hours, we then build in a quick review at the start of the next meeting. And now, at last, we find that things get done!

So, these are early days, and next week, Becky, one of the floor Supervisors, is leading the meeting. It just so happens that Michael is coming in to visit us. I've asked him if he wants to come in with us to experience our new meetings, and with a little trepidation in his voice he has said he will.

Who knows what might happen at the next Divisional meeting?

Chapter 6 - Problem Solving

I was slowly nodding off on the couch. It had been a long day at the Store and here I was, looking after Juliet and her brother and falling asleep at 8.30!

An issue that had been a concern for a long time and with which I didn't seem to be getting anywhere had bothered me a lot that day. Although I knew it was there, it had dawned on me that the bottom line for a lot of the business performance challenges I was facing could be resolved with the right type of staff. I just wasn't recruiting them and the ones I had who were filling the role really well didn't stay for very long. The main problem seemed to be the loss of staff members to other businesses on the retail park where my store was located.

Sleep summoned and I began to drift, the TV became a blur and then all of a sudden I was wide awake. Something had stirred me and I couldn't get clear what it was. There it was again – a little noise, a sort of giggle, but I couldn't make out from where – I got up to investigate further, and in the kitchen, standing on a chair to reach the chocolate milk, was Juliet, and alongside her was her brother. Juliet said, "He was thirsty, so I said I'd help him get a drink!"

So I helped Juliet get the chocolate milk and satisfy her brother's thirst – Juliet felt she should support him as well and enjoyed a glass full of her own!

"OK guys, it is way past your bedtime and I think we had better get back upstairs." I hurried them along.

They needed to clean their teeth again, of course, so that took another few minutes. Miles went back to bed and straight to sleep, but, as I expected, Juliet was now wide awake, "Have you been to sleep at all?" I asked her. "Well, just for a little bit, but now I'm not sleepy at all." She said rather unnervingly – I was in for a lengthy session settling her in again.

"You look tired." She said with the perception and directness that only a precocious eight year old can deliver. No emotion, no judgment – pure observation. So I told her that I **was** tired and that it was a busy time at work. "You can't get enough people to help you there can you?" Juliet suggested.

"No, I can't, how do you know that?" I replied, curiously.

"Well, Mummy came home last night and said that she had three short in her team and that people kept leaving. She says that it seems an impossible task to get the right people at the right times – and to stay."

Juliet said the last bit as if she was quoting exactly what her mother had said and she put on a strange face trying to show how her mother had said it.

"Why do people not want to come to work with you?" She persevered.

It was a question that had been challenging me for a long time and it came down to just a few things. One was the salary which we were offering; another was the hours of working that was unusual in my store (we worked late shifts into the evenings, because we stayed open late) and perhaps more worryingly was the problem that even those who had been around for a long time had been drifting away, eroding our level of experience and expertise.

"Why would someone want to work for you and why would they stay anyway?" Juliet, now with the bit between her teeth, was not going to let me off the hook and I started to wriggle in my seat. I didn't know the real answer to this.

I thought I knew, indeed I assumed I knew, but actually, I hadn't really asked the question very often, and perhaps more to the point, I hadn't done much about what I did know. I had taken little or no action to resolve this situation. However, it now dawned on me that I could take some positive action to do more - much more about it, than I had in the past.

"Why, really, don't they want to work for you?" She persisted. Why indeed. What was the real truth here?

We had been trying to pay people more, through using all sorts of devious schemes to beat the internal pay system, yet we didn't seem to be solving the problem. Maybe pay wasn't the problem - or at least the only problem. The key to this was that I didn't even know.

I was trying to solve the symptoms rather than find the cause of the problem. It was like I was going into a pharmacy with a sore leg and them just giving me a cream, any cream, without finding out what was the cause of the sore leg. In those circumstances, that would be absolutely crazy – it could be one of a dozen reasons.

Unless they asked me for more useful information, the chances of me getting the right product were very unlikely, yet here I was in a very similar situation plastering cream on the 'lack of staff leg' without knowing what the cause was.

I needed to know more about this.

The steps I needed to understand this better were:-

- Identify what the symptoms were
- Check who they applied to
- Look beneath for the real cause
- Use those affected to provide real solutions
- Check that the solutions don't cause any other problems in themselves
- Try the solutions
- Review what we've learned

The next day was my day off and as it was a nice day, I decided to take a walk and allow some of these thoughts to percolate through whilst I was walking. I enjoyed the rhythm of walking and being out in the fresh air and at one with nature, so to speak, enabled me to become really creative in my thought process.

I recalled the evening before and it just seemed more and more clear to me – I had been fire-fighting with this issue and desperately trying to paper over the cracks, without realising that I needed to find out the real reason behind my loss of team members and an inability to recruit.

I realised too, that this would need me to be honest enough to admit areas where I myself might have to change – that would be a tough call for me, as I was used to being the 'boss', and whilst I didn't always believe I was right, I thought I **usually** was.

What if I was challenged on a point like that?

What's more, this is a technique that I could use again and again with members of my team and even better, it would bring them on board with their ideas and input to build my relationships with them.

Then we could get even better results, because they would see issues through the eyes of the real world, rather than just from my perspective. I would let them decide, but it could be the 'Getting to the Bottom of Problems Team'. As a to start with random name anyway!

Right then, how best to proceed back in the business?

Perhaps I could pull together a group; a varied group of people who could start to thrash out an activity that we could apply to any problem situation?

Actually, just doing this was a challenge at the moment, because we were so short of people that we couldn't actually manage the business itself, let alone have loads of people away from the sharp end. So, I decided to be radical!

So I put a notice up asking for the help of anyone who wanted to work - in a new, special way - to help start quickly solving the problems we were all experiencing.

I would pay for a room and food in the local pizza restaurant (again!), together with overtime and costs of getting home. I said that I would come to explain how this could work, that I wanted honesty and great ideas (and all ideas were great ideas!), and that I was determined to move mountains to get this sorted out.

I needed six people, would take the names of ten and the extras could be reserves.

There were 10 names up before I got into the Store the following day! They were all people who had shown concern (sometimes very loudly!) to me in the past – which was a great level of commitment already.

So, how did it go?

Well, the first thing to tell you is that they didn't want me around to work it out for themselves! This was my first test and so I suggested that they have some ground rules, which they agreed.

Rather than my own suggestion of the 'Getting to the Bottom of Problems Team", they decided to call the Team the 'FAST' Team, which was 'Fixing All Store Troubles' (FAST) Team, so that stamped their ownership on it.

They wanted license to meet for up to six times, weekly on the same evening each week. They wanted all ideas to be considered, but they would test them against the following measures before they submitted the ideas.

- Will it fix the problem permanently?
- Will it be ethical and legal?
- Will the costs be value-creating overall?
- Will it cause other problems?
- Will it really work? (they put that in as well as number one to ensure that they double-checked themselves).
- Is it important? Or is it urgent? How to deal with both?

...and then I left them to it.

Up to now, the team have solved 13 different problems in this way – and there have been many other team members involved in these FAST teams, so much so that now, we have very few problems –– we call ourselves the 'Problem-Free Zone'!

In fact this is being delivered with such a fine art that small groups fix things permanently on the hoof – through little informal groups who I hear around the place. I just don't get 'problems' brought to me any more!

And this from Juliet asking, "Why really, don't they want to work for you?"

Oh yes, you're asking, what were their solutions to the recruitment issue?

To start with, there were five: -

1. Create a questionnaire for existing staff to answer, which listens for the truly important things, which real people want from their jobs and build on what they need to be happy, challenged and safe.

2. Ensure that everyone understands what they are supposed to do, that they are trained properly and that they openly give and receive feedback in every way you can think of.

3. Find out when people are bored and find out what they would like to learn about.

4. Encourage people to have real and regularly available buddies when they start with the Company.

5. Look at some new ways to recruit people to work for us. A separate team worked on this for 5 weeks following the first team – it was decided that this was just too big a topic to handle with

the main one and yes, they did find some radical ways to recruit new people to join us (one of which involved me being on television – but that's another story!).

My Key Points on Problem Solving

Choose People Who Know

Involve those who the problem affects, in finding out the real reasons for the problem and the real solutions. They are motivated! So use their energy and get them involved. They will also be very, very efficient in deciding what will and what won't work.

Let Them Loose!

Give them the freedom and your total trust to play with the problem and be radical, with a few ground rules. My role is to encourage and smooth out hurdles that get in their way, and benefit from their creativity. I made sure that I 'got out of their way'.

Get to The Source

Really grind down to the lowest levels of the problem. I now encourage them to be very, very honest – even if it challenges me. Will solving it make it go away permanently? Try asking 'Why" five times. At least, that's our way nowadays!

Give Them Some Tools

There are many 'problem solving' tools that can help people. Simple things like 'What if?" or the 'Ishikawa Fish' are often fun and compelling for people new to simple problem solving.

Keep Focused

Be sure to park other unrelated issues which surface and create a new team to sort them out if necessary – maintain the energy and focus of the initial problem. Ask 'What is distracting us here?' if stuck.

Does it Work?

Really test solutions to ensure that they fix problems permanently before introducing across the board. Be determined and honest, even if it means you will need to redo some of the work. Allow very open challenge to ensure success. And after it has been deemed a successful solution, review what happened.

Ironically, involving people made a big difference to the staff losses in itself. Indeed, three individuals came to me over the next two months and said that their involvement in the FAST team had stopped them from leaving!

Chapter 7 - Time Management

It was Rosie and David's wedding anniversary and we had been invited over for a little get-together of friends at their house.

It was so cool to feel that as Rosie's boss, she felt able to include me in her circle of friends, despite the challenges we had faced together. We were excited to get over there and enjoy the company.

Juliet, as usual, was quite the life and soul of the party and was busying herself as the 'hostess with the mostest' and generally helping out with the hors d'oeuvres and spending quite a little time being admired and thanked by the guests. Steve and I gradually blended into the party and said hello to quite a number of folks we knew vaguely, but who were rather Rosie and David's friends rather than ours.

After an hour or so, I was surprised to find that Juliet was nowhere to be seen and it seemed strange that she wasn't playing her part in the crowd. I decided to investigate! I went around the house and still there was no sign of her, so I decided to have a look upstairs, where there were people milling around, as they made their way to and from the bathroom.

Juliet's door was closed tight shut and I knocked gently on it and asked if she was on there. There was no reply. So I knocked and asked again. Still no reply. I somehow felt that she was in there, so I gently opened the door and tiptoed in.

Juliet was lying on the floor of her bedroom on a thick red rug that was beside her bed. She was staring up to the ceiling.

"Hi Juliet, are you OK?" I said.

"Of course I am!" she said and then she said no more.

OK then, how to handle this? From experience I knew that Juliet would have good reason for lying on her floor. So as I felt in a rather special place whilst she continued to look at the ceiling – in a sort of way that she didn't seem to mind my presence, but kind of wanted to continue to the end with whatever it was she was doing. Obediently, I complied and sat quietly on her bed watching, although out of her sight.

Suddenly, she got up and stretched herself out. She then said, "I was having a 'thinking moment'." As if I was supposed to know what that was and what it meant.

"Sometimes, if I have been very busy, I need a bit of space and time to think straight, otherwise, I might burn myself out". I had to stifle a smile at that point, not out of disbelief or disrespect, but more about the very grown-up way that she had said it.

It was as though I was the mad one for not being able to understand the simple logic of what she was saying. "I don't want to become too stressed out."

Unless you have had the opportunity to hear words such as these from the mouth of a precocious child, you won't be aware of the great paradox in what you experience. On the one hand, you hear the wisdom of a bright, yet razor-sharp grandmother, and then you hear see the physical presence of the child.

What you see definitely isn't what you get! It's as if there is a total mismatch. I needed to know more about this new side to add to the already many talents of this fascinating child.

"So, what were you doing on the floor," I asked.

"Well, I was just switching myself off for a little while and having a bit of a rest."

"What do you mean you were switching yourself off?" I asked, wanting to know more.

"Well, sometimes I need to stop thinking about 'stuff' and think about nothing, and the best way that I can do that is by lying on my floor. It might not work for everyone," she clarified, for me.

She continued, "I find that if I clear my mind and stop thinking so much, so often new and fresh ideas and solutions come into my mind. The less I think about something, the more I'm empty, leaving space for the good stuff to come!"

Hmmm – I felt a little puzzled here. "So do you do this very often Juliet," I asked her, with fascination regarding the reply, yet to come.

"I try to do it every day and sometimes more than once, if there is a lot going on," she said.

"And what is the purpose of this?" I asked, again expecting a short and terse reply.

Juliet waited a moment or two, as if to collect her thoughts. "I like to hear the quiet in my mind sometimes, and by coming up here and looking at the patterns on the ceiling I forget all the 'stuff' that is flying around."

"What do you mean by stuff?" I questioned her once more.

"Well, in this house and with school and Brownies, there are such a lot of 'things' to think about, so sometimes I need to refresh myself by not thinking of much really at all, and then quite often a little idea comes into my mind which allows me to do something I've been struggling with."

"I call it 'My Time' and I use it when I think it is impossible to do anything else and I need to look at things differently," she casually added.

"Anyway, let's go back to the party, I want to see if Mum has got to the desserts yet, that's my favourite bit." And off we went!

So we made our way back downstairs and mingled with the party. Later on, I saw Juliet with the biggest piece of chocolate cake, almost bigger than her face, but she seemed able to cope with it well!

We continued to enjoy the party, and at the end of the evening, for it was a Friday and the children had been allowed to stay up until late, we said our goodbyes, and "Thank you" to the whole family.

As was usual, I was working at the Store on the Saturday - our busiest day of the week - and with Rosie being on a day off, no doubt to clear the remainders of the festivities the previous evening, it was all hands to the pump on the sales floor, with all the key people working closely with the teams to make the best service available for our customers.

So, it wasn't until Monday, when I was having a really challenging day in the Store, that I thought of the experience I'd had with Juliet and tried to make something of it. Actually, and to be honest, at the time I was so busy that I gave up trying to make some 'My Time' and left it for the moment.

When I got home that night and thought a little about the experience with Juliet and then the lack of 'space' I'd had at the store over the last couple of days, that I pondered on what it meant.

There was no doubt an element of 'can't see the wood for the trees' syndrome about how we worked at the moment, and often we were pulled backwards and forwards between issues, giving none of them the time they deserved. There seemed to be no simple way forward. Then I remembered exactly what Juliet had said about it – and they were her precise words too.

"When I think it is impossible to do anything else and I need to look at things differently."

I wondered what she meant by this. I often thought about things from a different point of view and then still couldn't find a solution.

But then, in a moment of inspiration, I realised that what I was doing most of the time, was making a judgment about the situation, which was true in just my eyes. A personal judgment and then deciding on the ways forward based just on that.

I needed to challenge any assumptions I was making – and that was what Juliet meant that she used her 'My Time' for. She had found there were other ways to see things by simply creating clear space and thinking little about the issue at hand.

The other thing I had figured out was that there seemed a need to stop doing some things in my life to enable me to really focus on the important things – like I had attempted to fill the days with, as Juliet would have said, 'stuff' and not the important things in my life.

So how could this look in practice? I had realised that there was no reason at all why I couldn't make sure that I managed some 'My Time' into my days and that most of the other elements of what I'd learnt from Juliet came from this – creating thinking time.

I had assumed that I had to work myself as hard, if not harder than the rest of the gang. Whilst I wasn't going to sit there all day with my feet up, there was a great opportunity to enable more people to do the things that I didn't need to do, which would free me up to move myself and the team all up to the next level of achievement.

That achievement could also include some, if not all the elements of what I was getting from the business and how that impacted on my life.

Suddenly, I remembered that this was where I had come in. The whole trigger for this series of learning about how I worked with my colleagues in this business came about following my conversation with Juliet in the first place and how she felt after the times when Rosie had come home and felt frustrated with her life at work, and how I had been the precipitating factor here.

I needed to get this clear in my mind: -

- I can create as much space in my life and work as I need to, by doing the things I'm there for and the things I'm good at. Anything which is a struggle for me personally, I can find and develop someone else for.

- I can use the time that has been freed up to think through the issues in the business and create an environment where we can all flourish – where the folks I work with want to come to work and we can make great business and have fun.

- I can use some of this time to flush out any of the false assumptions I've been making.

- I can take some time out alone or with my team which removes us from the hustle and bustle of the day to day operation and think off-site sometimes, as we've started to do.

- I can 'lie on the floor' and let answers come to me in 'My Time'.

Whilst these were all interesting ideas, how was I actually going to do it?

The first thing to do was to assess, virtually minute by minute, what were the things I did which someone else could do. If I found myself saying 'They can't', I would ask, 'What could happen so that they could?'

When I started to do this, it was an absolute eye-opener and I found that in truth, there wasn't very much at all that I did that others could not do. What was left was a load of stuff like, leadership, vision, coaching, future planning etc.

It involved me shaking off a few things that, frankly, were things I'd held onto because of history – maybe I'd let a little go in the past which had come back to bite me.

One vivid example was where I'd rushed off on holiday and left someone with a report to complete. I recognise now that, because it went wrong and it ended up with me being hauled over the coals for it, I'd always held onto such activities tightly ever since.

The real truth here was that I'd left someone unprepared who had done the best they could with inadequate coaching from me.

This was one of the things I would 'let go of' as soon as I could.

By the end of the week I had a hit list of tasks which were either 'nice to do' for me or better done by others. There was also, and I found this rather difficult to admit to, a number of things, which I didn't need to do at all. There was a further phase to this. I was able to find quite a chunk of pieces of work I'd given to others to do; yet I'd never acted on them and they were doing them unnecessarily.

It was like spring-cleaning my workload and that of my team. Make no mistake though, I had to really test it out very carefully indeed. In fact I went as far as checking my retained list four times in all. The challenge became what I didn't need to do, which, by the end was rather fun!

Once I'd begun, the team started to notice and asked me questions. I explained that I was having a purge on stopping doing stuff. I was delegating, over a controlled period of time or even better, stopping doing some things at all. I was really careful not to 'dump" stuff on the key players and I took them on board in the process, to ensure that they gave me good feedback, to make sure that they were comfortable with what was happening.

...and then my management team started doing it themselves!

They came up with a staff survey where they asked every one of their teams the following three questions.

1.   What wastes your time?

2.   What do you need?

3.   What could you do?

The results were both alarming and fascinating and we let them get involved in the delivery of the changes we had needed to make, but had not really appreciated.

It came down to false assumptions again. Like: -

They can't do this

They won't want to do this

They aren't capable

They won't be good enough

There is no time for them to do it

They have other things to do

It's not their job

I need to do it myself

These were the basis of the assumptions we had been making and there were a lot more too.

In the end I had to stop to take breath – there was a wealth of space becoming available – now the challenge would be how best to utilise it.

Over a period of three months, as a management team, we were able to give ownership to our team members for over 65 activities. From key-holder rosters, to organising the staff room noticeboards. From feeding back key information, to analysing stockholding figures, and more.

I was able to support and coach each of my key supervisors in a number of the tasks only I had 'been able' to do previously and so, eventually, I began to feel like I was able to create space for me to consider the next challenges.

It came to me as a series of upwardly spiralling performances, where we had on-going challenges not precipitated by complaints or under-performances of work we had carried out, but actually by the self-challenge of owners of the new responsibilities.

These guys were challenging themselves every so often, to see if they could do it even better than they had up to now. Even when they had got to perfection they went back again!

I found myself being challenged (!) by owners of task responsibilities because they wanted to change the process. With a little trepidation, I was able to accept their changes in procedures, with just a couple of provisos.

Was it going to be better and not make other problems and that we had to remain within the corporate image? That had to be a given, or we might have had total anarchy!

And what did I do with the time? What indeed!

I Became a LEADER!

My Key Points on Time Management

Delegate and Develop

I delegate often! This saves me time and is a great development tool for others to learn from. Quite early on, I realised that it also helps build the relationship with my people and kept them interested and challenged.

Say 'No' More Often

These days I take full responsibility for all I take on. I say 'No' more often! Now, I try to make decisions on just how much I will accept from others and within what timescale, by being honest and resolute, above all, with myself. People's perceptions of me have quickly changed and it is getting easier and easier to say that 'No'.

The 'Closed/Open-Door' Policy'

By all means have an open-door policy for people to speak with you – and I **do** close it sometimes. That gets my projects done and gives me mental space to give quality time to people when needed. I think it's a great model to the rest of my team too.

Stop Doing Stuff!

I started to think about whether an activity is value-creating one or not? It really is as simple as that. If I only had half the time in my week, what would the real priorities be? That really started to define what the most important areas of my work are. I realised that to make progress, the decision whether I would choose fighting fires all the time or to seek the real causes and sort them out forever was the criteria I would use.

Finding 'My Time'

How do you do this, in your busy schedule? That's what I wondered too. So I started to think closely about how I spend time. Then more and more, using some of the new ideas I'd had above, I focused on creating the time to think. To find some space, so I take walks – to process. I think if you can do this, you'll surprise yourself.

Go Home On Time!

What? I'm a Leader! Yes, some of the time I am! And I help people shine by doing more, by doing less.

So I take my breaks. I go home on time to enjoy my leisure time – 'My time'! I make sure I spend time with Steve and, now and then yes, I take a walk on the beach. And I always take my holidays. I try my best to keep sharp and be refreshed. I might sound like a bit of a renegade, but why not?

Chapter 8 - Half Time

The meal was over. Now it was time for the presentations. Each business had been asked to create a presentation to support their nomination for the title. Suzanne and her team were fourth out of six to go.

The first group sang and danced along to that great Yazz classic 'The Only Way is Up' and received rapturous applause, especially when as an encore, they distributed copies of the words to the audience and got them involved in the experience too. They would indeed be great challengers.

The second group took it in turns to comment on what being in the competition finals meant to them. It was moving and emotional, especially when one of their team broke down in tears, as she told the riveted audience that this was the first ever time she had represented anything in her life. Strong candidates again.

The third group took it upon themselves to walk amongst the audience asking individuals what they thought of their store business. Careful preparation had ensured that they chose people who knew their business well. They had been invited to visit, see and talk to many of the team not present on the night. They were compelling advocates of the nomination.

For Suzanne's team, who came next, there was a surprise. Instead of the whole group taking the platform, as with the other teams, no-one appeared. Gradually, all the lights dimmed until there was no light at all in the place.

Suddenly, there was laughter and giggling over the PA. A rectangle of light appeared at the front of the room, growing in size from a small dot, until it was the size of the screen on the wall.

The shot pulled back until it was clear that we were hearing, and now seeing, a team meeting in a room. Some of the members of the meeting were present in the audience, others not. There was a structure of the meeting and one of the lesser staff was encouraging the group to get to the bottom of the problem.

The shot moved around the room looking in the faces of the participants. They were happy, supportive, creative faces and comments, which flowed from the mouths on those faces, matched them. Great open ideas, new thoughts and what was more, supportive and helpful suggestions building on an idea, rather than finding fault.

Switch to the storeroom, where merchandise was being received from a lorry. People were busy, but laughing as well. They were supporting each other; there was a general air of working together, working for each other and offering to take action.

Fast forward to the Christmas party, where everyone had taken the trouble to dress into costume. There were many people having great fun and joining in. There was a little sketch where a group played out a sort of pantomime with a song made up from the latest Company commercial tune.

And what was even better, great fun was had by all.

As the presentation ended, there was a huge rush of applause. Each of the representatives who were present in the audience stood and bathed in the spotlight, which flashed erratically around the room. For the finale, the lights dimmed again and in complete silence, there was a short cameo of one of the team and a customer - both were roaring with laughter.

This was no sterile commercial transaction; this was a relationship. The closing shot remained on screen, a still from that last short clip. Both the customer and staff member laughing heartily together!

It was a strong image to close on.

The fifth group ran a customer service role-play, where unsuspecting members of the audience were chosen at (a sort of!) random and dressed in wigs and dresses (the men certainly!). They were then offered scripts to read and handled expertly by members of the team. There was a really strong message of customer understanding and delivering beyond expectations.

The sixth team chose a sort of quiz show format, where they flashed multiple choice questions on the screen behind them and then had members of their teams answering in a rather mocking way.

It was going to be too close to call.

Chapter 9 - Team Building

It was a cold and damp Saturday morning and the field was wet underfoot. This was the traditional weekend away for the Brownies at the end of the summer – their very last outdoor event before the winter chills sent the group indoors until the spring.

I was there at Juliet's express invitation and when she saw me arrive, she rushed over to say 'Hi' and to introduce me to all of her young friends.

It took but a minute before she rushed off to the central area of the camp where the other patrols were congregating.

This was an overnight Friday stay for the campers who, unusually, were not just the troop of Brownies, but also one or more of each of their parents. So looking rather bedraggled and a bit on the pale side, if I might say so, as were both of Juliet's parents and her brother! They had clearly enjoyed the overnight stay.

I remembered what the outdoor life could be like from my Girl Scout days and on the rare occasion where Steve suggested we might take a holiday under the stars. I felt that strange sensation, which was a mix of cold, damp, nightmare, very early rising in the morning and a deep feeling suggesting that a nice hotel would be better!

The whole point of the weekend was for the parents to join in and they were allocated to the individual patrols of which their daughters belonged.

So the team worked together as parents and children and attempted to win the various activities, which were set up around the field. Some of these were physical activities, some were games and others were skills.

Just on 11 o'clock, the whistle blew and the troop assembled in formation to start proceedings. Fortunately, as an invited guest, I was here as a general observer and supporter for the team I wanted to follow – clearly that would be Juliet's, which was the 'Elves' patrol!

I watched fascinated as the exercises were described and each of the patrol leaders were then assigned into a rotation of several of those activities, with each team attempting to score the most points.

Juliet, who was the 'Elves' patrol leader, was therefore in 'command' of her girls and a set of adults, a challenge in itself, so I settled - feeling in need of a cup of hot chocolate to keep the chills away - to watch what would happen.

I don't know if I was suddenly becoming super-sensitised to my life, but I certainly had started 'noticing' a lot more going on around me and as I watched, I was struck by the performance of Juliet as a leader.

The first thing she did, was to ask everyone to be quiet whilst she explained what would need to be achieved, saying that if anyone had any questions, she would try to answer them at the end, if they could let her have one complete through.

She explained very calmly and clearly for so young a girl, that she would try her best to be fair with everyone, that to win she would need everyone's help and that she wanted everyone to have fun, try their best and that would be good enough. That was all she could ask for.

She then went through the exercises in more detail from the pack of information she had been given and at the end took questions. Whilst she answered some of them herself, some she didn't know the answer to and she asked two of the girls to take notes.

At the end she sent the two girls and a grown up off to the adjudicator to find out the details. She explained that she had chosen those two because they were always very careful and clear in activities back in the meetings they held each week.

They had three activities to complete during the first exercise and they had one hour to complete it.

Then she asked for volunteers and more especially for those who would enjoy each of the three activities. That sorted out most of the patrol and there were one or two who didn't mind, so Juliet allocated them for some specific reasons.

One because she was tall, one because she was good at writing and the other because she could go with her sister, who was new to the group and perhaps needed a little more support, because their parents couldn't be there.

The group dispersed, each team with about 8 members, a good mix of parents and children in each.

Juliet nominated one person (and, interestingly, always a Brownie) to lead each group, explaining to them that it was very important to be clear and explain what they needed to do. I also noticed that she told each of the leaders, 'You can do it and win us lots of points'.

There was an enthusiasm about the leaders that they then took back to their teams. I also noticed that each of the leaders that Juliet had chosen were positive and whilst excited, fully focused on the activity to be achieved.

After this, I saw Juliet checking in on each of the teams as the hour progressed. She was checking that they were OK and also giving them lots of encouragement and not criticising.

It was clear that each of them loved working in partnership with Juliet, and also how she was able to leave them alone to get on with their activity in the way each of their teams wanted to. If one of the team members came to Juliet with a question, unless sent by the team leader, Juliet was careful not to answer the question herself, but to send them back to their own team leader to ask them.

Juliet's patrol didn't win – but they were second!

And what I did see, was that Juliet's team had the best time - truly the best time! They were so happy as they collected the runners up prize (a large box of chocolates which they all shared out very rapidly between them!).

So just what had I seen Juliet do?

- She had been clear about the goals and the instructions (the ground rules)
- She had made it clear that she needed them all to help her
- She had left the teams to work out their own solutions
- She had trusted the teams to deliver the best result they could

- She had appreciated the skills of some of her people and worked them to their strengths

- Everyone felt valued and part of a greater contribution. They were a team

- She had made it clear that they were allowed to have fun together

- She had supported the team's leaders by:-

1. Being there if they needed her

2. Not countermanding their decisions to their team members

3. She had sorted out the problems that held them back (like the incident with the string which ran out in one activity)

As usual, this young lady had given me, more than 20 years older than her, a lot to think about and relating what I had seen to the business I managed was going to be challenging and fun.

Whilst it would be useful to have a few thoughts now about it, I had other things to do before Sunday evening, and it was only then that I tried to draw from Saturday's experiences and overlay them on my work and team.

Over the past few months we had started to make real progress within the business. This was not least due to the understanding I was being able to draw from hearing what Juliet had to say. There was, however, a lot more to do.

At the start of this journey, the team were not together as I hoped they would and it really was down to me to ensure we worked ourselves through this problem and come out the other side as a far stronger unit.

We were currently a team of individuals and whilst I didn't subscribe to the ethic I had often heard that 'There is no 'I" in TEAM'. I did believe the one that said, '**T**ogether **E**ach **A**chieves **M**ore'

I felt it important that I valued the individual contributions and enabled each of the team members to knit together when they needed to. Thus a strong team with strong individual skills making a total stronger that the sum of its parts.

Yes!

My Key Points on Team Building

Get to Know Your People

Only by regularly talking and listening to my people did I have any chance of getting to really know them. Who they are; what they bring; what turns them on and what really interests them. So nowadays I do this informally as well as formally and I really do have the sort of close relationships with my team that benefits everyone.

Value Everyone

Great teams are made up of different sorts of people and all bring something to the party. I've learnt to enjoy the benefits of the mix and I can see that it is bringing many benefits. It's about appreciating what 'different' people can bring to the team? Trust each other - and be trusted.

Have a Clear Common Goal

We now work together to clarify and agree what the goal for the team is – and everyone having an input is vital and creative and synergistic, so we make the time and space to do it well. I'd say that today, we revel in the benefit of a collaborative workplace environment.

Create a Working Framework

I've had to put some thought into **how** we work together. I know a lot of factors depend on this. Virtually; meet occasionally; meet every day or week? Whichever, we have begun to make it clear for each of us, because some members of the team will need a tight framework, some less. For most of us, we have agreed up front so that everyone knows what each other wants.

Give Overall Direction

My job, as I now see it, is to get clear what the 'What' about the job, the reasons; the value; the outcome. And then let the 'How' go – to let it flow from them. I definitely enjoy a far greater reward in the outcome now that I do. And we are creating an extraordinary team too.

Support is Personal

Some of our team like to keep in personal touch regularly, some occasionally and even those who might just want to turn up on the day with the result (scary, but they are around!). I watched for what **each** individual needed – it became a strength of mine – and I know that I'm getting the best from everyone now.

Chapter 10 - Customer Service

When the coach arrived, everyone was excited. The trip had been arranged for months and the grown-ups and the kids were all ready to go to the City to explore in their own way, the delights which were promised.

There were quite a few of my team going along and it had been a juggle to get the shifts worked out so that those interested could be freed up to make it.

It was an early start, but the whole coach-load was complete in good time and they were on their way.

Rosie and I were geared up to take Juliet and Miles to the big shopping malls and then onto the wide-screen cinema, which was showing the latest kids' movie. They were both very excited.

But first the shopping.

As a special treat, Juliet was to be allowed her own money and to shop for several things for which she had been saving. Some were to be clothes for her and others were to be gifts for friends' birthdays which were coming up – it was a kind of 'growing-up' for her.

She was going to go alone into shops and carry out the whole transaction herself.

First stop was the clothes shop she had been talking about all the way there. Rosie let her go inside and waited patiently outside the shop as she went about her business.

After 15 minutes, Juliet came out, looking very disappointed. There were none of the clothes she wanted in her size. Rosie decided to go back in with her and check.

She came back and confirmed that Juliet had been right and there were none of her top choice dress available. Very disappointing.

The next shop was the second choice, but Juliet had a spring in her step as she made her way to the checkout area with her purchases. There was a very long queue and when she got there, she was treated as if she wasn't there, with others pushing past, just because they were bigger. I watched her for a minute and leapt to her defence. The assistant seemed to be disinterested, but took the money.

Outside, Juliet was excited about her purchase, but the first thing she told Rosie was about the treatment she had received, which seemed to have upset her.

In the next shop, Juliet was luckier. An assistant asked her if she needed some help, in a very smiley sort of way. Juliet wanted a particular colour tee shirt and the delightful girl spent quite a time listening and talking to Juliet. She even asked about the 'adventure' of shopping on her own. The helpful young lady even walked her to the door and waved goodbye!

For her final purchase, Juliet was not exactly sure what she was looking for. And she fell lucky once more, with a delightful older lady assisting her, who had a granddaughter of Juliet's age.

Again Juliet was thrilled with the help she received, especially when the lady was on hand to help her decide, after asking Juliet exactly what it was she wanted and even treating her as a normal customer! It was great to have someone else to tell you just what looked right.

Rosie was delighted with the last two purchases and even more the attitudes of the helpers that Juliet described.

Of course they enjoyed the rest of their day and the movie was an equal measure of squeals of delight and screams of fright. Young Miles seemed to show few signs of fear!

Everyone was tired on the coach and there were some sleepy-heads - and not just youngsters!

On the way back, I reflected on the experiences of Juliet. In some ways it had been a gentle baptism into the world of being a customer, these days becoming more and more challenging!

So, there had been some interesting contrasts and I was not going to miss the opportunity to learn! It seemed, on initial inspection, to be quite easy.

- Make sure that what you sell is what people want
- Make sure that it does what it says
- Make sure it gives value
- Value = Quality x Price

OK, so that had the availability and 'does what it says on the tin' sorted out – now what about buying it?

- Have people to take money as quickly as customers want it to be

- Enable them to judge whether to build a full relationship or give them speed
- Have them watch for when people could benefit from help
- Build trust such that customers will take their advice
- Enable fun to be part of the deal

I shared the experience with those who had been out with us, and others in the team.

It was almost a mark of what customer service meant to us, that without prompting, they decided to get together smaller teams to identify what customer service meant and what would they would all look to do differently in the future.

For me, once again (this was becoming a habit!), I gave full license to the teams to do what they wanted to make our place a more attractive experience for customers.

There was a routine measure that we used in the business as our customer satisfaction measure.

The team decided this to be too unwieldy; so some of them took it upon themselves to design questionnaires that they would use to find out for themselves what customers really thought.

In giving away the control, of course I still felt a little awkward – in truth, our people knew best, from their own experiences. They could remember instances from years ago.

One person had not shopped in one particular store for over 25 years, because of a poor service she had experienced just once. And she regularly told people about it too – what kind of damage had that day so long ago done to their business over the years?

So, with the help of half a dozen or so of the team, we worked out a way to collect information on the worst experiences and the best experiences from our own people to add to the 'research' and finally, after much thought we came up with the following points: -

My Key Points on Customer Service

Wear Your Customers' Shoes

Actively seeing your 'offer' from your customer's perspective will help you. I've included all of my team in this now too. Together we encourage each other to 'be the customer' and experience what we offer to our customers from the outside in. Every customer has individual needs, so we work hard to ensure that we always appreciate this.

Stop Your 'Systems' Getting in the Way

However important our systems are to our business, as far as possible, we remove all trace of them from the salesperson/customer interface. We've had a look at how we can free up our key 'selling' people to do just that and not suffer the mental interference of 'other tasks to do'. I encourage the team to bend the 'rules' for their customers. And they love it!

Have 'People' People Sell for You

Where we can, we now get people who can talk easily to customers to sell our products or services for us. We give them the freedom to create relationships; to be 'friends' with our customers and to simply have have fun with them! I have always remembered that experience of Juliet's and how it might have been different with some of the people who she encountered.

Everyone be Customer Focused

Whilst not everyone will be customer facing, I encourage everyone to have this question in their minds in every activity they undertake

'How will this help deliver the very best service to our customers?'

From back to front of the organisation to be customer oriented.

Welcome Complaints

Complaints are an opportunity to over-deliver in response to an initial problem. Although we try not to get too many of course, getting complaints solved really, really well, is huge fun and, we've found, a magnificent opportunity for our store to show itself off at its best ironically! We learn so much from the feedback and we often develop new, strong and valuable relationships with the people we've helped!

Chapter 11 - Managing Change

I took the call just after 9pm. On the end of the line was a loud, noisy and very excited caller, who I listened to for a few moments to let her get back down to earth - but just a little.

Once Juliet had given me her initial outburst, I asked her to tell me again, because I hadn't really picked out much of use, the first time round.

"We're moving house," she said, "and going to live on a mountain! I'm going to have a pony and a field for her to run around in," she added, with more excitement. I waited to ask her more as she excitedly explained to me how wonderful it all would be, as they moved to the country and lived a life I knew that Rosie and David had always wanted, both for themselves and the kids too. It would be just great for all of them.

Juliet was so excited, yet I knew that she had so many friends in her area, from school, to the Brownies and then through to other acquaintances - kids like Juliet did not seem short of friends.

"Well, that's so cool," I said, "Where are you going to live then?"

Juliet thought for a moment, and then told me that they weren't 'actually' moving far, just the other side of the City, but it was quite a big City and the distance was quite a way, home to new home.

Rosie came on the phone then and we got talking. Things were going much better at the Store now and I know that was one of the precipitating factors of the move. Work was a lot less stress, so they could focus on something they'd always wanted.

"So I'm going to have to look for a new Supervisor then, am I?" I said, joking. "You'll have to try a lot harder than that," she said, "We aren't going that far!"

In fact for Rosie, I reckoned that the journey to work might even be easier, a factor I knew she would have been considering as they made their big decision. For the kids the changes would be more significant.

Two days later, I heard from Juliet again. This time she was a little more sombre.

"I'm going to need to change school, move to a new Brownie pack and the friends I have close by will all be gone – I'm not sure why we ever wanted to go there." She started sobbing. It was dawning on her what the changes might mean. From the exhilaration of the first call to this one was quite a difference.

"Hey, so what about the mountain and the pony and the countryside?" I said, trying to be helpful.

"Yeah, well, it's not going to be much fun without any friends, is it?" was her response. Oh, dear!

I caught up with Rosie at the Store the next day and asked her how the plans for the move were going. She confirmed that although all the plans were going well, Rosie and Miles had started to experience the potential downsides and were feeling a bit sorry for themselves.

I shared my thoughts about when I moved once when I was a child, and we agreed that the emotions were running high at the moment, yet, both of the kids, and the family as a whole, would settle down to the new experience, once they'd got used to it.

Rosie told me that they were getting both the kids involved with the move, so that they were able to help with the decision about which house to choose, which school to go to and also, from time to time, they intended to take them to the new area and to get used to the place.

A couple of weeks went by and I met up with Juliet and Rosie in the shopping centre where we worked. It was lunchtime and I was invited to join them for coffee and milkshakes (for her!) nearby.

I asked her what was happening with the house move and as usual, Juliet was her more-mature-than-her-age self.

"Well, I've been thinking a lot about this," she said, "And this is what I've decided."

Here we go, I thought!

"There are lots of things which I will miss about our house where we live now and that disappoints me, but it has been fun here and so I will remember that.

"There will also be lots of things to get used to in the new house and where we are going to live and that will be a bit of a challenge for a while (see what I mean about being beyond her years!).

"But all in all, I think we will have a lot more fun in the new place when we get there – Mum and Dad have let me and Miles help them decide on the new house, which is real fun. And next week, we are going to look at schools and we will have two to choose from!"

Juliet had taken the time to reflect and think this all through. The excitement was back!

"So, all in all, what do you think about moving then?" I asked.

"I think it will be better, once we settle in and there will be lots of new opportunities for us all."

And with that, and those slurpy sounds you get when you get to the end of your milkshake, it was time for her to be off, shoe-shopping with Mum!

Change, then. It's what life is all about. What was that great saying I once heard?

'What kind of man would live where there is no daring? I don't believe in taking foolish chances, but nothing can be accomplished without taking any chance at all'

Charles Lindbergh

We were about to embark on a series of reviews of workload in the Store and it would mean change for many of the people, in fact almost everybody. I was due to make the first announcement the next day.

What would it mean to them all? How would they take it? What ideas could I glean from Juliet to help me make it work best for them?

Well, I decided that I would give them as much information as I could do, in general, about the reason for the changes. Many would be worried about what was going to happen, so I would then schedule one-to-ones with them all just as soon as I possibly could – a tall order, and they deserved it.

The next step would be to encourage each and every one of the team to help us work out the program of change to try to get the right outcome, but be flexible with the 'how' we were going to do it.

This meant that although I had a clear picture for them to understand in terms of the result, they would help me, with their involvement, understanding and skills, to make the best effort at what actually would happen.

I would give up my attachment to some of my thoughts and ideas, to enable their ownership of the solution.

Some of the people wanted to express their concerns directly to me and I was happy to be there for them. I was also careful to explain exactly why the changes were happening and I was pleased that I had taken the time and trouble with the planning of the whole exercise.

I knew what I needed to do and I stuck to that, working evenly and fairly with everyone. There was no room for favouritism. There was no flexibility outside the actual needs of the business being achieved.

I stuck to my guns – even with those who were prepared to shout the loudest and moan the most (and I have one or two of those!). I knew that if I weakened and gave in to one, then there would be many more behind.

Some people came back more than once and demonstrated those classical avoidance tactics when change is in the air. One blamed 'Head Office'; one said they 'didn't care'. Another wanted to know why someone else had got one deal and it couldn't be offered to them (we had real business reasons for that). And there were others.

Frequently I was told in hushed tones that some weren't being reasonable, even though we were and to 'ignore them'. It seemed that I had the majority on my side.

Over the next couple of weeks, we carried out all the briefings and set up small teams to try to work out the best solutions for the individuals concerned.

Every member of staff was involved in some way – and I mean every one – no-one was missed. They not only appreciated the input each of them had but, you know, some of their innovative solutions really were fantastically helpful for all.

A number of people came forward with their own needs, often far and away from what the rest of the management team and I had expected. These often created the flexibility, which helped us. Their solutions were magnificent, creative and interestingly, often very caring.

We ended up with a series of team solutions, which worked well for almost every individual. There were one or two who we just couldn't accommodate and, yes, we had to let those people go. We did this in as caring and supportive way we could. Indeed, with a couple of leavers since, we have taken back one of those who left us.

As far as I was concerned there were several tit-bits of feedback I received, some directly and some posted on the feedback board anonymously.

All were positive (except one of the anonymous ones). They made comments about their involvement, that they hadn't expected positive to come from this, but it had, that they had some new challenges, which they were looking forward to.

That they were proud of the way these big changes had been handled and that they thought I was great! I had five of those!

And the negative one – well, oddly it was from someone (and I think I know who it was), who said that they didn't like being involved, they just wanted to be told.

Oh yes, and finally – we washed it up as a management team a few weeks later – to learn about what had gone well and maybe what we would do differently in the future.

We learn all the time nowadays. So here are some ideas...

My Key Points on Managing Change

Change Happens

The world we live in is constantly changing. I think that's such a cool place to be! How exciting and varied and stimulating, if we choose to see it that way. As a leader, I have the skills to switch on this viewpoint in my people. And it is such a wonderful thing to see!

People Resist Change

This change thing is OK, as long as it happens to someone else – and not us. As people resist change, they have many tactics that they show up with to deny their involvement! It's about fear of the unknown. It's scary – and it's important to recognise this.

Give Them Time

I now see how people are different and react differently to change. Some engage with it immediately and love the possibilities. Others see only problems. Change is like a smaller version of grieving. And people need time and space to be with that. I've learnt that I must not lose these people by only focusing on the positives, because for some that is not what they want to hear about – they need support and 'to be heard' too.

Stick to the Plan

I took the time to plan change carefully – where possible, in collaboration with all of my team - and I have checked and double-checked that it **is** value-creating and will work. Whatever comes, in the main I keep confident with where we are going and stick with it – whatever the resistance.

Communicate Change Well

One thing I now do, is to get change information to people quickly and openly. I involve them as much as I can. I speak in clear language and allow for questions and that I will always respond if there are queries – and I **make sure** that I do.

Be Available

Then, sometimes I need to be available to explain the change on a one-to-one basis. Some of my people want to know how change will impact on them first, way beyond everybody else, so I have to be available. I've found that I have to understand their concerns and also be firm as well.

Chapter 12 - Coaching and Feedback

It was a lazy Sunday afternoon at the new house. Rosie and David had invited us round for a superb lunch and now we were just chilling out and chatting. I was delighted at how far we had come in the business, and Rosie showed that by how she was responding in her new home.

As I watched Juliet playing with Miles, I was really interested in seeing just how she was interacting with him. I don't know if the experiences I had been having were making me much more sensitive to being around Juliet, but in this instance, it was not how she was reacting with me personally, but more about what I was observing from a distance.

Miles had dug out a model plane, which he had received for a previous birthday or Christmas or something, and together they were having a close look at how it would need to be assembled.

With most kids, this would possibly prompt a series of minor arguments about who wanted to do what (especially when it came to applying the glue!), but on this occasion it was interesting to observe just how Juliet was handling her brother.

Before they had even started, she had taken him upstairs and shown him where it would look great hanging from his ceiling and I heard her say, "Wouldn't it look just the coolest, having it hanging down here, can't you just see it?"

Clearly Miles had become really excited about it and she then cleared the spaces while he went and got the fun bit, the model kit from the cupboard.

She then reminded him of how great the model would look when it was done and hanging up in his room, and then showed him how the finished model would look if it was done 'properly and carefully' as she cautiously reminded him!

Between them, they then tipped out the box of parts for the plane, and she told him that one of the things she found useful was to put the parts on the table in the order in which they would need them. She was careful, I noticed, to let him do it, with just the odd, 'That's right'' or 'Just here' to help him on his way.

Miles spent the next few minutes separating the parts and sorting them out.

Over the next hour, she gradually helped him to understand the instructions, yet was very careful to let him do the work and learn the best way to get it right. Every so often she held it up as it grew and asked him what he thought about it. At about the hour mark, there was something of a disaster, when a wing was put on upside down – yet, this seemed to be another opportunity for Juliet to help Miles learn.

"What did we do wrong?" she said. And Miles admitted that he'd not been watching properly and had been distracted when a piece got turned over to apply the glue. "It's my fault, I've spoiled it," he said, starting to get really upset. At this, Juliet consoled him and said, "Let's have a look at it now and see what we can do about it".

Gently she helped Miles tease the two parts apart, as the glue was still tacky. That done, they quickly reattached the parts in the right places, and the job was resolved.

"Now, I wonder how we can stop that from happening next time." She said. Miles said that he would pay attention better for the rest of the afternoon – and he certainly did, keen for there to be no further mistakes.

Juliet was quick to encourage him by saying. "It's always good to realise where you went wrong, so that you can remember for the next time".

Pretty simple and also quite profound!

There were also a couple of moments where Juliet showed Miles what to do, so that he could then have a try himself afterwards, but Juliet kept this down to a minimum. Miles did most of the work.

Finally, after an hour and a half, Miles formally announced that the model was complete. It would take a little longer to dry, he said, but gingerly he brought the completed model over. Juliet's action was to admire the result from afar and let Miles enjoy the result.

It was only when he had slowed down a little that she suggested that they take it upstairs to have a look at what it might look like in place. This they did, and Miles came downstairs really excited about what the finished article would look like in place in his bedroom.

"When do you think you'll be able to paint it?" Juliet asked Miles. "Tomorrow, after school, but it might take me two nights," he replied. And so it was agreed.

A couple of evenings later, I was passing their house, so I thought I would pop in and see how it was doing. Juliet greeted me and called for Miles to show me the completed airplane.

He literally dragged me up to his room to show me, and there it was, hanging precisely as in the picture on the box. Delicately hanging by the fine threads that Rosie had provided. It looked fabulous!

Of course I was not going to let an opportunity to learn from my 8-year old professor pass me by.

It struck me that sometimes, I tried too hard to 'do the doing' and stood a little too close to those in my team. I realised that Observing, Supporting and being Clear, were more important than hand-holding.

That my people were all different and they would all benefit from different levels of support. Some, like Miles, would be OK most of the time, yet I knew that there were others who would need much closer help.

But that did not need to be only me. There were others in my team who could do some of that too. And, of course, as I actually did less, I would have time to give more support where it was needed from me.

And they would become more proficient; more flexible and above all, more confident in what they felt capable of - even more so than they did now.

Later that week I reflected on what I'd seen, and it came down to the following thoughts I had: -

My Key Points on Coaching and Feedback**

A Coaching Environment Creates Time

Coaching is a true win-win! I've realised I would win though developing my people by coaching, because it frees me up for other more important 'growth' things. By encouraging them to be the best they can, my people win, through taking responsibility, becoming more motivated, feeling fulfilled and enjoying huge personal growth.

Coaching Provides Better Solutions

How can I have all the best answers? I can't. Working in collaboration, where I challenge individuals to share their opinions, ideas and perspectives, creates for truly great solutions. I've given up some of my personal input and listened more, enabling others to fully contribute.

Individuals Grow Magnificently!

Creating success through coaching people, means that their confidence builds as they find their own solutions to their challenges. It is **their** solution. They start to realise – 'Hey, I can do this!' ...and do more - much more - than they ever imagined possible.

Organisational Culture Expands

On the back of the achievements of a few, a cultural shift happens. Solutions - brilliant solutions - come thick and fast. My job becomes creating the best value from it all. Through watching Juliet, I saw how I was able to let my people go and make more of themselves, with just a little nudge or two from me!

Feedback is Good for All

It's really valuable to make time for feedback to be natural, regular, consistent and even informal. We each encourage positive feedback, especially recognising a good job done. I help the team make 'learnings' out of mistakes. We try to be 'blame free', strongly encouraging out–of-box creativity and risk-taking, without the fear of reprimand.

**Note. Over time we changed 'feedback' to 'feed-forward', where the goal is to learn from what has happened and help each other become even better the next time. This helped some of my team understand it better and use it much more.

Chapter 13 - Managing Performance

The journey had been such a challenge over the last few months. But what a magnificent time we had all had. The business was growing beyond expectations and the people were just shining through. Instead of a struggle, going to work was beginning to be a wonderful thing!

There was one last issue facing me in completing the foundations for my progress. It was an area that bothered me, and I wanted to ensure that I had the insights I needed to help me through the next stages in my development. It would also be of huge value for those of my people I wanted to encourage and help them realise their potential too.

I needed to be a bit better at managing performance.

At last, I was finding myself in full alignment with Rosie as the year unfolded, so we arranged to have a day together. This time, she came over to my place and we sat down to have coffee and a chat. Relaxing together, at last!

Rosie was so thrilled as we started to talk, because she had been to Juliet's half-year review with her teacher the night before.

"We have these meetings twice a year formally - in the middle of the first term and at the start of the third term. But Mrs Edmonds is talking to us informally all through the year.

"Juliet is doing so well. In most of her subjects, she is in the top 4. There are a couple of areas that clearly aren't her favourites - or strengths - and her teacher says that is completely normal."

Rosie took a moment to consider her next words, "In fact, Mrs Edmonds had a really interesting view on how we can help Juliet be the best she can."

We each took another sip of coffee, as she continued, "She says that whilst it's important to get a rounded education, what is even more vital is that we encourage Juliet in what she really loves to do. She believes that when students are passionate about something, they will naturally excel."

I was able to catch up with Juliet later in the week and as I congratulated her on the results from her review, I asked her, "How are you able to get better and better all the time, Juliet, it's every term that you do so well," I laughed.

"Well, it's not very complicated," she reproached me, before carrying on, "I decide each term what I'm going to learn and then I do it, with the help of Mrs Edmonds, of course."

That seemed simple enough. Then Juliet continued, "Sometimes what I do doesn't go so well, so I learn other ways to do it, and she helps me see that." She thought a little more, "I ask her if I need anything to help me and she usually finds a way to get things for me. Well, not everything, of course!" She laughed.

"And often, she asks us who we would like to work with as well. Sometimes she agrees and so I have learned from other children. Other times, she has me work with someone I can help, which is really nice to be able to do too. Mrs Edmonds is good, because she seems to know who to put with whom.

"All the time, she is talking to us all and making sure we're OK with anything we are doing. It makes me feel good when she tells me so and I know I can ask for help with what I am doing, when I need to.

"Above all, whatever I achieve, I know that it's been me that has done it. If I haven't, it's been me as well!

"At the end of term, I look back at what I've done with Mrs Edmonds and I feel proud of it because I was the one responsible for it. And that's such a nice feeling."

On my drive home and for the next few days too, I thought about what Juliet had said.

I realised that one of the things I had been doing was trying to make all of my team equally good at everything they do. And that now seemed not logical at all.

I also reflected on some of the leaders I'd worked with who had inspired me to better my performance and I thought of 3 key people (not all managers!) who had tactics that had really worked well for me.

I could also think of several more, on whom I will not dwell, save to say I didn't exactly thrive with them!

I found that when I performed best, there were usually several key elements to the relationship. If these were present, then I got even better. If they weren't, then I wasn't motivated at all, so my feeling about myself - and my performance - dipped. And it was almost always the relationship that made the difference, which was really interesting.

And I was delighted to know that this was something entirely - and only - under **my personal control**. So, no excuses!

The first thing I needed was clarity about what was expected of me and this to be consistent. If goals were changed, then it needed to be discussed fully and openly together.

I needed challenges that stretched me just enough, with the level of support I needed. Then I needed to be able to try things out for myself, without the fear of being found 'wrong'.

One manager explained to me the value of learning from mistakes and being sure that I made some (as long as they didn't bankrupt the business!).

I needed to be clear that it was my responsibility and mine alone, to get better at what I did. There was no blame on anyone else, it was down to me.

Then I had to have the right perspective for the decisions and actions that I took. Again, encouragement to be comfortable to 'not get everything right' (was what one manager had told me!) was OK!

Another challenged me to help myself by really understanding what the purpose was for all I did. Then I could measure decisions and actions against that before I took them.

Having this aligned would is invaluable to achieve all my goals and if anything feels out of line, then that is a good 'gut-instinct' for where I wasn't going to be my best.

Above all, the people who mentored; coached; supported and drove me forwards were those who showed me a level of respect that made us equal. This they did by listening; following up; being consistent with me and asking for help themselves.

I learnt this a lot throughout the last year, because I needed my people and I needed them with me as completely as I could.

As a real, live, partnership.

Somebody even told me that it's important to always respect the person and manage the behaviours, for they could be developed and, as long as the person was and felt respected, they would respond too.

Thinking back to what Juliet's teacher said, I'd found that I did even better in my role when I did what I liked to do as much as possible, which meant that I had to delegate more of things that I wasn't so good at.

And I found that often, there were people in my team I could develop too, by giving them types of work I was not so good at myself. Playing to their strengths, not mine, was a goldmine, once I realised it.

So, for my team, and in summary, I found the list below gets to the point quite nicely.

My Key Points on Performance Management

Keep it Simple

There are many and varied performance management schemes and templates around. Why make this complicated? We now get better buy in and overall value from a quick and simple process, which everyone understands and uses.

Value the Person

Mostly everyone sets out to give their best at their work. When performance suffers it is not usually the person – it is something lacking like confidence, training, skills or experience. We try to understand this and manage the performance of the behaviours, not the person.

Play to Strengths

The best performances come when individuals are in the 'flow'. This is always when they are doing what they do best. I have learnt to focus on more of helping them be even better at what they are already good at and less 'remedial' work for those few areas where they are less strong.

Make the Time Regularly

Like I do with Michael, I know that my own people value the time I spend with them. So now I see a large part of my role is to make time available. By helping them grow, by hearing them in our conversations. I have started to create regular time for them and make the time **fully** theirs, interruption and distraction free.

Give Away Responsibility

I encourage others of my key staff to get involved in measuring performance. I've taught them the skills and ensure that they use them to my high standards. I have seen them grow just by using these skills. And everyone is responsible for their own development.

Approach Consistently

My employees need to trust me. So consistently applying performance measurement is very important to us all. This also means that when tough solutions have to be applied, I must apply them consistently to everyone too.

Delegate and Develop

As individuals evolve and grow, I'm delegating to them with confidence those activities they can handle well - even better than me perhaps. My freed time can then be better used for my own focus – on growing my own leadership role and skills.

And, of course, all of my people will gain too. "

Chapter 14 - Outcomes

As Suzanne finished speaking, the meal with her team the previous week was coming to an end. She had been talking to Michael for nearly two hours. He had a clear picture of where her team had been and come to and her remarkable story.

And now the finals were here, the presentations had been done and it was time for the judges to do their stuff.

There had been six judges, from various levels of the business. There were a couple of general staff, some middle and then some senior management.

Whilst the presentations had been one element of the proceedings, each of the judges had made a report about all of the Stores in the final, following personal visits. So each Store had received, over the last month, a visit from each judge.

That had been the acid test and had enabled each of the Stores to show off their performance as a business, how they worked together with their customers to deliver satisfaction (and beyond).

And equally, how they worked as teams within each of those businesses to grow, support and nourish an environment of opportunity, for the staff, for their customers and ultimately their businesses overall.

So the 'tests' had been rigorous!

The Managing Director came on stage and the audience hushed. As usual there were a few thanks to pass on, a review of the overall business of the group in the year past (and a few hints about how things were progressing so far this year).

In reverse order from three down he announced the winners.

Suzanne's team did not feature at either 3rd or 2nd and there were some anxious looks around each of the people from her store present in the audience.

When it came to the winner, he made the following comments: -

"The winner tonight comes from a group of people, the like of whom I have never witnessed before in one of our Stores. This is truly the most supportive, excited and passionate team of people that I have seen in my 28 years of business. I am even more impressed by the way they have overcome challenges over the past year, to really delve into their solutions and have worked together to deliver an outstanding set of results financially and indeed in all the measures we have in place.

My recent visit to the Store in question proved to me that there is a way for individuals to be challenged - and supported - in such a way that they love their work. They look forward to every day they face the hostile world in which we trade these days. Business is a war-zone out there, yet in this particular store, this team has got it just right. They are an example to us all."

Suzanne and her team were holding their breaths collectively, as they considered his words, as a team. They had come a long way together and they had had their ups and downs over the past year. Was this the business he was describing?

Was it to be their year?

The MD continued, "I am delighted to be able to make this presentation tonight to this brilliant team and the person who has inspired them. Not wishing to take anything away from every individual member of the team, I have been so impressed by the determination and focus of the leader of this team.

"The person in question has certainly shown how they are able to learn and develop on the hoof, with good spirit and steel. They have also shown enormous innovation in how they have got there and found inspiration from the strangest of places.

"So, yes, to Suzanne and your team, I now understand and applaud your secrets. And ask you to join me on stage for the presentation."

By the time his final words came out, it was not possible to hear a word he was saying. There were six ecstatic members of Suzanne's team leaping and screaming towards each other for a team 'hug'. Michael was in there too and many, many others who knew of the successes they had achieved were passing on their congratulations.

They were just so delighted as they took the stage.

Suzanne had the opportunity to say a few words.

"I am just delighted to receive this award. I feel privileged to be able to stand here in front of you, with just a few of my people, to say thank you so much for choosing us! It would have been great to have everyone here together, but I know that would just not be possible.

"I would, of course, like to say a big thanks to everyone who has worked in our team. Everyone has been there for each other as we have learnt and shared so much together in the last year. In many ways I have not been their leader, I have been led by them. We have delivered success by consensus and working together.

"I'd like to thank Michael for being so supportive and understanding. I know you hoped we would come through and your supportive management of me, especially in some of the tough days I faced at the beginning, has to be a model for other area managers to follow. I am grateful for the space you gave me to share my fears and the encouragement you gave me. You are a great boss and I know that you have learnt with us."

Suzanne took a deep breath and continued, "I'd like to thank someone else who has been very special to me over the last year. I have learnt so much from the unexpected wisdom, the fun and joy and sheer magic of this person.

"I wouldn't wish to identify her in person normally, but many of my team have come to understand that we can learn so much from those around us.

"A clear inspiration came to me early on when Juliet, the daughter of a key member of my team, explained to me how she felt some days when her Mum had had a tough day at work. I learnt from her that as managers, we have a responsibility to understand that the workplaces we provide for our people are so much more than the 9 – 5 (and the rest!) job.

"Our workplaces affect many others connected, however loosely, to our people. With that in mind, I and my great team set about changing the way we work so that every day at work is not a dread, but it is, in its own way, a great place to come and spend our time."

We have fun, we work with the customers and each other, to have fabulous relationships. I set out after that first conversation with Juliet, to understand better what I do and what I can do differently. Juliet has, through being who she is, not only a child, but an example, shown me the way."

In finishing up, Suzanne had this to add, "Perhaps we could all take a leaf out of her book and watch, notice and listen to our children for ideas and encouragement. Indeed, I have learnt that it is not only children; not only Juliet I can learn from; but there are examples everywhere that I can draw parallels from and use in my work.

"If I have one word of encouragement it would be this. Be observant, notice things and use those things to apply or at least try out things differently. You may, like I have, be surprised...

...by what I learnt from a child."

With that, the rear doors of the room burst open and the rest of Suzanne's team poured in to join in with the celebrations.

And high on someone's shoulders, beaming and thoroughly enjoying herself, was Juliet – sharing in the success for us all. A success which, only by being completely herself, she had helped to bring about.

Chapter 15 - Bonuses and More!

If you would a free, instant download of "10 Leadership and Management Articles You MUST Read", where you will find varied pieces that will tweak your thinking and have been read by over 200,000 in the field of management and leadership, go to **martinhaworth.com/extras-1**!

I will be creating a series of eBooks over the next few months. Some are written already and some are still being researched.

Bearing in mind that this book is the first (March 2015), it might look a little thin at the moment, but you can find what is there right now at: -

martinhaworth.com/books

I'd be delighted to let you know when they do come out and, where possible, offer you the opportunity to get them for free, for a very limited period.

Just go to **martinhaworth.com/extras-1** and you will be added immediately, so that you get early advice of what's coming next (and you'll get those free articles too.

Chapter 16 - And Finally

I hope that you have found these words useful and practical to apply to your organisation. If you have, please be kind enough to support a new writer with a review on the book's Amazon page.

Thank you in advance. I really appreciate that you have taken the time to do this.

Suzanne works within the retail arena – a very focused segment of industry.

Will these Key Points work where you work as a manager and as a leader?

Of course! Everything in this book is about working with people and if you work with people, with a few minor adaptations, every one of these Key Points will work for you.

Try them out, one a day, one a week; become competent; teach them to others. You will indeed accelerate yourselves to fabulous success and without doubt you will become a great manager, maybe the greatest ever.

The idea of Juliet's story came into my life a bit crazily at 4am on a very warm morning one July and was the catalyst for Suzanne and me. It started with the idea that managers have a huge influence on the lives of the people in their teams - and beyond.

When we observe; when we notice; when we challenge ourselves to be better by doing things just a little differently.

None of the people in the book are individuals that I know. They are drawn from many wonderful real life people I have met and worked with over the years.

Everywhere, those who learn from Suzanne and Juliet will continue their work in their enlightened workplaces, making the wonderful difference for their people and the hundreds and thousands who are touched by their positive experiences.

There are many Key Points in the book, but don't sweat them all at once. Just try some on now and then and learn as you go.

You see, there is one more Key to this. And that is you!

Being a 'Suzanne' kind of Leader in your workplace is such great commitment – so honouring to your people. Share yourself with them – they will appreciate it.

Managers are in a truly unique position in the world and you can use your influence to make the world a better one, by being a truly great manager, for yourself, for your organisation and for your team. Feel free to contact me with your successes at: -

martin@martinhaworth.com

I look forward to hearing from you and wish you lots of fun in your development!

About Me

I spent my working life at the 'sharp end', working for a major UK retailer and managing businesses large and small. And, in many ways, I miss it!

I loved the excitement of working with people and even in the most challenging circumstances found that through working with the people, there was great individual potential just bursting to get out.

To everyone's benefit.

I feel privileged to have worked with those thousands of people and that in some small way, with at least some of them, I was able to turn them on to their own latent, yet magnificent abilities.

I am a graduate of CoachU and accredited as a coach with the International Coach Federation.

I live in England and my websites are at: -

MartinHaworth.com

CoachTrainLearn.com

Best Regards
Martin Haworth
Gloucester
England

www.ingramcontent.com/pod-product-compliance
Lightning Source LLC
Chambersburg PA
CBHW070820180526
45168CB00002B/692